YOUR KNOWLEDGE HAS VALUE

Francis Marete

Thematic and Critical Discussion. Quantitative and Qualitative Research

GRIN Verlag

Bibliografische Information der Deutschen Nationalbibliothek:

Die Deutsche Bibliothek verzeichnet diese Publikation in der Deutschen National-
bibliografie; detaillierte bibliografische Daten sind im Internet über http://dnb.d-
nb.de/ abrufbar.

Imprint:

Copyright © 2013 GRIN Verlag GmbH
Druck und Bindung: Books on Demand GmbH, Norderstedt Germany
ISBN: 978-3-656-73363-8

This book at GRIN:

http://www.grin.com/en/e-book/279487/thematic-and-critical-discussion-quantita-
tive-and-qualitative-research

GRIN - Your knowledge has value

Der GRIN Verlag publiziert seit 1998 wissenschaftliche Arbeiten von Studenten, Hochschullehrern und anderen Akademikern als eBook und gedrucktes Buch. Die Verlagswebsite www.grin.com ist die ideale Plattform zur Veröffentlichung von Hausarbeiten, Abschlussarbeiten, wissenschaftlichen Aufsätzen, Dissertationen und Fachbüchern.

Visit us on the internet:

http://www.grin.com/

http://www.facebook.com/grincom

http://www.twitter.com/grin_com

Thematic and Critical Discussion

In quantitative and qualitative studies, a distinction can be seen between critical and experimental approaches when conducting data analysis. Both approaches inculcate a form critique for a particular research. In most cases, experimental approaches are meant to identify the participants' experience and their different perspectives. It is also meant to understand participants' thoughts and ideas, practices and feelings from their language use, whereas the other one does not. Critical approaches, however, conflict with experimental approaches about mainstream research among other variations.

Thematic analysis, though rarely known by researchers is widely used method in both qualitative and quantitative analyses. These articles argue that this method of data analysis offers a theoretically flexible and accessible approach to both qualitative and quantitative data analysis (Boyatzis, 2008). Thematic analysis is thus a flexible and useful method used to analyse both qualitative and quantitative data.

"A tale of two Cultures" depicts how some social scientists argue that there exist some similarities between quantitative and qualitative methods of data analysis. In the article "A Tale of Two Cultures", James Mahoney and Gary Goertz show that these two paradigms are made up of different cultures. Each paradigm is coherent, internally yet identified by contrasting practices, norms and toolkits. They introduce and outline the major differences that exist between the two traditions which touch almost all aspects of researches in social sciences. Such aspects include goals, designs, concepts and measurements, casual effects and models, case selection and data analysis (Boyatzis, 2008).

Their arguments have mainly focused on differences that exist in quantitative and qualitative research. The two authors also wish to increase exchange, toleration and learning by scholars. They make this possible by enabling them to reason outside their own culture and see a different scientific world view. The book is written in a simple and easy style. It also contains various examples from real world to show different methodological points.

Gary Goertz is a professor of political science who takes the same at the University of Notre Dame. Among his works is a *User Gide to Social Science Concept*. On the other hand, James Mahoney is a professor of Economic History at Fitzgerald. He is also a professor of sociology and political science at Northwestern University. His works include *Colonialism and Postcolonial Development*.

"A Tale of Two Cultures" is a must read, especially for social scientists. It best suits a group of social scientists who specialize in one research culture in preference to another. The book provides concrete examples to illustrate the background of the two cultures. If a researcher needs clarification on different topics on research methods, the book may be particularly relevant. It gives a clear guideline on different issues with the "two culture approach". The book also appreciates and promotes exchange of different research methods. It provides a clear insight on the interconnections that exist between different research methodologies (Mahoney, & Goertz, 2012).

"A Tale of Two Cultures" depicts how quantitative research has, for many years, been seen as an ill-mannered stepchild in the field of quantitative research. This belief is then hampered by the belief that qualitative research employs primitive analytic techniques and numerous dislocated enthusiasms that are used to elaborate cases (Mahoney, & Goertz, 2012). The book challenges this stereotype by illustrating the distinctiveness that exists in quantitative approach. It also avails not only an accessible but also a comprehensive challenge to different critical conventional views.

This work is meant to give readers insight the reason why conflicting approaches in social sciences are the best when one is given goals and assumptions between the two paradigms. It also gives a room for readers from the two sides to understand other alternative perspectives for them to reconsider their own goals and approach. Therefore, it is clear that "A Tale of Two Cultures" introduces a clear challenge to basic fundamentals of how research should be conducted.

According to Wesley, most courses and textbooks in political science methodologies do not show much attention to analyses involving qualitative documents. Most of them concentrate on interviews, qualitative and quantitative analysis, field studies and experimentation. Only a few concentrate on quantitative document analysis whatsoever. When studying qualitative analysis of political texts, the study is broadly categorized as archival or unobtrusive research. It may also be conflated using coding of field notes or transcripts (Wesley, 2010). They also lack detailed methodological discussions which are a bit disconcerting. This is based on the condition that most of these political scientists have combined shreds of textual interpretation as depicted by their studies. Such analyses should be guided by the rigour of the same level as those found in the quantity fields.

The article has a number of guidelines that compare these methodologies with traditional models. These models were used to analyze various quantitative contents. It also gives a summary of a few quantitative document analyses and examines other same approaches in other disciplines of social science (Wesley, 2010).

Wesley subdivides the study into three ontological perspectives. The first perspective claims that qualitative and quantitative traditions are designed to be ontologically distinct such that they are incommensurable. Different scholars believe in hard-and-fast connections that join tenets of positivism to quantitative methods on one hand and interpretivism and qualitative method on the other (Wesley, 2010). The second perspective holds that both qualitative and quantitative methods are taken to be commensurable in line with the positivist approach about social life. The study shows the difference between qualitative and quantitative traditions are particularly stylistic and are substantively and methodologically unimportant. The third perspective holds a middling perspective about the interconnection between qualitative and quantitative research methods. "Dualists" unlike "purists", value collaboration that exists between qualitative and quantitative researchers. Dualists also see the importance of their interrelationships (Wesley, 2010).

"Qualitative Methodology and Comparative Politics" article tries to review the position of qualitative methodologies in comparative politics. The maintain aim of the articles is to put more emphasis on the merits and the research contributions regarding to qualitative methods. In comparative politics an emphasis on the strengths of the methodology to be used is enhanced (Mahoney, 2007).

Qualitative exploration methods are highly used in topics regarding the study of comparative politics. Either authoritarianism or democracy can be pointed out when it comes to the above study. When formulating assumptions and methods used, qualitative methods can be used for enhancing substantial methodologies in ensuring efficiency. Rapid growth and development of different reliable articles about the comparative politics has been written to enhance its study.

A research has been carried out for the past five years showing that scholars have found it difficult to cope with the extensive developments in the study materials. Unlike researchers in other fields of political science, researchers in comparative science do not use well established programs while doing their research. These programs do not provide more reliable assumptions compared to the well-defined programs used by researchers from other subgroups of political science. Due to this weakness researcher from comparative politics are more likely to start their research with hypotheses that are not testable (Mahoney, 2007).

Codifying of the procedures used by qualitative researchers is among the greatest improvements in the case study of comparative politics. New hypotheses have been formulated by the researchers in improving the methodologies to use in their research. However, at times the outcomes observed do not conform to the predictions expected.

New hypotheses are formulated by the researchers in ensuring logical study of comparative politics. Creation of hypothesis is highly emphasized by researchers as it facilitates the study of the definable data and processes that helps in the study of comparative politics (Mahoney, 2007). Lots of emphasis is also ensured on the study of data and processes taking place over a period of time as the time differences in the occurrence of events are believed to be affecting the outcomes.

Similarities and differences in analysis are used in evaluating hypotheses in qualitative research. Although over the years different methodologies have been used by the researchers, many have testified that in their methodology similarities and differences are factors to consider in the creation of a material hypothesis. Researchers have come up with different methods of analysis in case studies involving comparative politics that best suits their methodology. Testing of hypotheses can be done using the researcher's case study features depending on the desired outcome (Mahoney, 2007).

Use of cross-case and within-case forms of analysis is highly recommended. This is because there are various desired cases with the appropriate features that make it most effective in attaining the required outcome. Researchers compare these two methods when they try to find the most appropriate method. After completing a research, they have to report the results of their findings and ensure that the readers are unaware of what sequential steps were taken in the analysis. "Qualitative Methodology and Comparative Politics", the two methods of theory testing can be combined with a more complex method.

References

Boyatzis, R. E. (2008). *Transforming qualitative information: thematic analysis and code development.* Thousand Oaks, CA: Sage Publications.

Mahoney, J. & Goertz, G., (2012). *A Tale of Two Cultures: Qualitative and Quantitative Research in the Social Sciences.* New Jersey: Princeton University Press.

Mahoney, J. (2007). Qualitative methodology and comparative politics. *Comparative Political Studies, 40* (2), 122-144.

Wesley, Jared J. (2010) "Qualitative document analysis in political science." *T2PP Workshop, Vrije Universiteit Amsterdam.*